First World War
and Army of Occupation
War Diary
France, Belgium and Germany

34 DIVISION
102 Infantry Brigade
Bedfordshire Regiment
51st, 52nd and 53rd Battalion
23 March 1919 - 12 July 1919

WO95/2463/4-6

The Naval & Military Press Ltd
www.nmarchive.com
Published in association with The National Archives

Published by

The Naval & Military Press Ltd

Unit 10 Ridgewood Industrial Park,

Uckfield, East Sussex,

TN22 5QE England

Tel: +44 (0) 1825 749494

www.naval-military-press.com

www.nmarchive.com

This diary has been reprinted in facsimile from the original. Any imperfections are inevitably reproduced and the quality may fall short of modern type and cartographic standards.

© **Crown Copyright**
Images reproduced by permission of The National Archives, London, England, 2015.

Contents

Document type	Place/Title	Date From	Date To
Heading	WO95/2463 34 Division 102 Infantry Brigade 51 Battalion Bedfordshire Regiment Mar-July 1919.		
Heading	51 Bedfordshire Regt 1919 Mar-1919 Jly		
War Diary	Antwerp.	23/03/1919	24/03/1919
War Diary	Wahn	25/03/1919	25/03/1919
War Diary	Lind	24/03/1919	17/04/1919
War Diary	Hennef	17/04/1919	30/05/1919
War Diary	Hennef	14/05/1919	14/05/1919
Heading	War Diary of 51st. Bn. Bedfordshire Regiment. From 1st. June, 1919 to 30th. June, 1919. (Volume 1).		
War Diary	Hennef	11/06/1919	18/06/1919
War Diary	Wahn	01/07/1919	12/07/1919
Heading	WO95/2463 34 Division 102 Infantry Brigade 52 Battalion Bedfordshire Regiment July 1919.		
Heading	52 Bedfordshire Regt 1919 Jly		
War Diary		01/07/1919	31/07/1919
Heading	WO95/2463 34 Division 102 Infantry Brigade 53 Battalion Bedfordshire Regiment April-July 1919.		
Heading	53 Bedfordshire Regt 1919 Apl-1919 Jly		
War Diary	Siegburg	01/04/1919	01/05/1919
War Diary	Siegburg	03/04/1919	30/06/1919
War Diary	Wahn	01/07/1919	31/07/1919

(4)

WO 95/2463
34 Division
101 Infantry Brigade
51 Battalion Bedfordshire Regiment

Mar – July 1919

51 BEDFORDSHIRE REGT

1919 MAR — 1919 JLY

EASTERN DIV'N.
W.D. I
51st Bn. Bedfordshire Regt.

WAR DIARY or INTELLIGENCE SUMMARY.
Army Form C. 2118.

(Erase heading not required.)

Instructions regarding War Diaries and Intelligence Summaries are contained in F. S. Regs., Part II. and the Staff Manual respectively. Title pages will be prepared in manuscript.

Place	Date	Hour	Summary of Events and Information	Remarks and references to Appendices
ANTWERP.	23/3/19	09.00	Disembarked and proceeded to Rest Camp.	
" "	24/3/19	10.00	Entrained for WAHN (COLOGNE)	
WAHN	25/3/19	02.00	Reached WAHN 02.00 25/3/19	
"	25/3/19	07.30	Detrained at 07.30 and marched to LIND. Billeted in huts at the Dynamite Factory. Orders to Antwerp attached.	
LIND	24/3/19	18.00	The following Officers reported for duty from 11th (S) Bn. Essex Regt.	
			Capt. J. C. Willet R.C. Capt. F. Coward R.C.	
			Lieut. F. C. Jackson Lieut. J. F. Dalzey	
			" V. E. Swait " H. Spices	
			" F. N. Butts 2nd Lt. C. J. Watkins	
			" A. C. Davies " A. F. James	
			2nd Lt. R. J. Mann " H. J. Buck	
			" J. Clayton " E. C. Milford	
			" J. C. Fitzhugh " J. G. Stark	
			" J. Matson " D. H. Emery	
			" G. F. Venus	
			" J. G. Carl	
LIND	28/3/19		Lieut. T. Wallace R.A.M.C. taken on the strength of this Unit. Lt. Col. H.W. Buck D.S.O. R.C. having proceeded to Conveying Clearing Station May J. Edwards M.C. assumes Command.	

Army Form C. 2118.

WAR DIARY
or
INTELLIGENCE SUMMARY.

(Erase heading not required.)

5th Bn Bedfordshire Regt

Place	Date	Hour	Summary of Events and Information	Remarks and references to Appendices
LIND	29/3/19		Lieut S.G. Bonning Beaco Regt taken on the strength	
LIND	1/4/19		April Lieut S.G. Bonning Beaco Regt proceeded to Dieppe Area for Demobilization and are struck off the strength Capt L. Rowlands Lieut C.E. Wait 2nd Lt. J. Earl 2nd Lt. A.T. Venus " " h.A. Mann " " T. Jackson	
do	do		Lieut Col. H.D. Enok DSO. M.C. having returned to duty from country clearing station BONN assumes command of the Bn. vice Major Ewlis, M.C.	
LIND	5/4/19		Rev. S.C. Rutterford C.F.v.B. having proceeded to CALAIS is struck off the strength of this Bn.	
	8/4/19		The following Officers have been accepted as volunteers for service with the Battalion. Capt. C.N.M. Butterworth " R.D. Hume R.C. " A.P. Materno M.C. Lieut C.E.G. Galsdwyn " C.F. Wace " F.G. Field " A.H. Selloy.	

Army Form C. 2118.

WAR DIARY
or
INTELLIGENCE SUMMARY.

(Erase heading not required.)

5½ Bn. Bedfordshire Regt

Instructions regarding War Diaries and Intelligence Summaries are contained in F. S. Regs., Part II. and the Staff Manual respectively. Title pages will be prepared in manuscript.

Place	Date	Hour	Summary of Events and Information	Remarks and references to Appendices
LIND	8/4/19		Lieut A.R. Hall to D.F. Smith 2nd Lt. P.F.A. Thomas " " J.M. Humby " " S.G. Betts " " D.A. Page " " E.N. Wilkinson " " E.J. Nightingale " " H.D. Bennet " " J.E. Clay. Lieut A.E. Harrison 2nd Lt. A.F. Middleton " " H.F. Plumb " " R.M. Heron " " R.J. Berridge " " T.J. Bacon " " F.T. Burton " " H. Thompson " " J.P. Jones	
LIND	9/4/19		The following Officers proceeded to No.1 Concentration Camp for Demobilisation and are struck off the strength of the Bn. Lieut O. Ward " A.C. Davies 2nd Lt. R.H. Emery.	
LIND	10/4/19		The following Officers proceeded to No.1 Concentration Camp for Demobilisation and are struck off the strength of Lieut R. Lambert. Capt. Jn. Tapley & C.	
LIND	14/4/19		Bn. moved to HENNEF	
HENNEF	14/4/19		Lieut Col. N. Allason DSO Bedfordshire Reg. having rejoined the average a@chmes command of the Bn. vice Lieut N. HENNEF to take up duty on the Outpost line.	

D. D. & L. London, E.C.
(A501) Wt. W.1771/M2031 750/c00 5/17 Sch. 52 Forms C2.10/4

Army Form C. 2118.

WAR DIARY
or
INTELLIGENCE SUMMARY.
(Erase heading not required.)

5/7 Bn. Bedfordshire Regt.

Place	Date	Hour	Summary of Events and Information	Remarks and references to Appendices
HENNEF	19/4/19		Lieut Col H. Guest DSO M.C.	
HENNEF	22/4/19		The following Officers having proceeded to Ho 1. Concentration Camp COLOGNE are struck off the strength. 2nd Lt. P Annis 2nd Lt R G Thorpe	
HENNEF	25/4/19		Maj Edwards M.C. Bedfordshire Reg having reported his arrival assumes the appointment of 2nd in Command vice Maj Gilmore with effect from 26th inst. inst.	
HENNEF	30/4/19		The under Officers having proceeded to No1 Concentration Camp COLOGNE to struck off the strength of the Bn from 30/4/19 inclusive. Lt. Col. W Allason D.S.O. having proceeded on leave Maj F Edwards M.C. assumes command of the Bn.	Major
do	do			

51st Battn. Bedfordshire Regt

WAR DIARY
INTELLIGENCE SUMMARY

Army Form C. 2118.

Place	Date	Hour	Summary of Events and Information	Remarks and references to Appendices
X See next page				
HENNEF	16/5/19		Lieut Col. W Allason DSO having rejoined the Bn. from leave, assumes command from 16th inst. inclusive vice Maj. J.H. Edwards MC	
do do	do		Maj. J.H. Edwards MC assumes the appointment of 2nd in Command vice Major Crohels MC from 16th inst inclusive	
do do	20/5/19		Maj. G. White M.C. assumes the appointment of Commandant Eastern Divisional School.	
do do	24/5/19		Lieut F.C. Clarke and 2nd Lieut F.S. Crowsley have today been transferred to the 186th Prisoner of War Company (L. of C. DANNES) and 184th Prisoner of War Company (No 5 Area) respectively	
do do	28/5/19		The undermentioned Officers of the Suffolk Regt are transferred to the 4th Bn. Suffolk Regt with effect	

Army Form C. 2118.

WAR DIARY
or
INTELLIGENCE SUMMARY.
(Erase heading not required.)

Instructions regarding War Diaries and Intelligence Summaries are contained in F. S. Regs., Part II. and the Staff Manual respectively. Title pages will be prepared in manuscript.

Place	Date	Hour	Summary of Events and Information	Remarks and references to Appendices
HENNEF	29/5/19		From this date inclusive (Authority Orders Dis. No. A 4069) Capt R.D. Hume M.C. 2nd Lt. G.N. Hickinson 2nd Lt. G.J. Nightingale	
do	30/5/19		The undermentioned Officer having reported his departure is struck off the strength of the Bn. with effect from 28/5/19 Lieut Col. H.W. Luce D.S.O., M.C.	
do do	14/5/19		"A" Coy moved to SIEGBURG.	

W. W. Luce
Lt. Col.
Comdg. 51st Bn. Bedfordshire Regt.

CONFIDENTIAL

WAR DIARY
of
51st. Bn. Bedfordshire Regiment.

From 1st. June, 1919   to   30th. June, 1919.

   (Volume 1)

F. H. Edwards.
                                    Major.
     Commanding 51st. Bn. Bedfordshire Regiment.
2nd. July, 1919.

Army Form C. 2118.

WAR DIARY
or
INTELLIGENCE SUMMARY.
(Erase heading not required.)

Instructions regarding War Diaries and Intelligence Summaries are contained in F. S. Regs., Part II. and the Staff Manual respectively. Title pages will be prepared in manuscript.

Place	Date	Hour	Summary of Events and Information	Remarks and references to Appendices
HENNEF	11/6/19		The undermentioned Officer is taken on the strength of the Battalion with effect from 23.4.19 inclusive Lieut V. LEE M.C. Authority Rhine Army no. A/306/1183 of 9.6.19.	
do	18/6/19		Battalion moves to ALLNER in preparation for an advance in the event of hostilities being resumed. Secret Orders for an advance in the event of hostilities being resumed attached (Spy No 22)	

F. H. Edwards.
Major
Comdg 51st Bn Bedfordshire Regt.

Army Form C. 2118.

WAR DIARY
or
INTELLIGENCE SUMMARY.
(Erase heading not required.)

Instructions regarding War Diaries and Intelligence Summaries are contained in F. S. Regs., Part II. and the Staff Manual respectively. Title pages will be prepared in manuscript.

Place	Date	Hour	Summary of Events and Information	Remarks and references to Appendices
WAHN	1/7/19		Battalion moved to WAHN	
	2/7/19		Capt. G.E. Mackeroy M.C. having proceeded to 103 Field Ambulance for duty is struck off the strength of the Battalion	
	6/7/19		2 Lt. Welford having proceeded to dispersal Area for demobilization is struck off the strength of the Battalion	
	11/7/19		2 Lt. Murnagh having proceeded to dispersal Area of demobilization is struck off the strength of the Battalion	
	12/7/19		Major L.H. Edwards M.C. proceeded to dispersal to take over the command of the 14th Bn. Sussex Regt.	

2 Lt B Wentworth, Capt Adj X tn L Chief
Comdg 51st Bedford R.

(5)

WO 95/2463

34 Division
102 Infantry Brigade
5? Battalion Bedfordshire
Regiment

July 1919

52 BEDFORDSHIRE REGT

1919 JLY

52ND. BATTALION BEDFORDSHIRE REGIMENT.

WAR DIARY.

1919.
July 1st.   Battalion left SELIGENTHAL at 10.30 hours, and arrived WAHN BARRACKS at 13.30 hours.
2nd.   Remaining re-enlisted men left for England.
3rd.   General Holiday on Peace being signed.
4th.   Platoon Training as usual.
5th.   Company Training as usual.
6th.   Brigade Church Parade. Service of Thanksgiving for Peace.
7th.   Battalion Route March.
8th.   Company Training as usual.
9th.   Battalion Route March, through PORZ and WAHN to Camp.
10th.   Platoon Training as usual.
11th.   Platoon Training as usual.
12th.   235 Other Ranks left by special train for COLOGNE Races.
13th.   Battn. Church Parade in Garrison Church, WAHN.
14th.   Platoon Training as usual.
15th.   Platoon Training as usual. C.O. Inspected best Section in each Platoon.
16th.   Platoon Training as usual.
17th.   Platoon Training as usual.
18th.   Brigade Field Day. Battn. complimented by General on its work in the Field.
19th.   General Holiday. Peace Celebrations in London.
20th.   Church Parade, Garrison Church, WAHN.
21st.   Company training as usual.
22nd.   Brigade Field Day. Battn. Left Camp at 07.45 hours, and returned at 16.00 hours.
23rd.   Platoon Training as usual.
24th.   Company Training as usual.
25th.   Company Training as usual.
26th.   Inspection of Barrack Rooms by Commanding Officer.
27th.   Church Parade, Garrison Church, WAHN.
28th.   G.O.C. Inspected Coys. on Coy. Parade Grounds, at 11.30 hrs. Memorial Service for Officers, N.C.Os. and men of the Bedfordshire Regt. who fell in the War - held in Garrison Chapel at 14.00 hours.
29th.   Brigade Field Day. Battn. left Camp at 07.50 hours, and returned at 14.45 hours.
30th.   Company Training as usual.
31st.   Holiday: Divisional Horse Show at SIEGBURG.

WAHN.
2.8.19.

C.E.Attlee Lt for   LIEUT-COLONEL.
COMMANDING, 52ND. BATTALION BEDFORDSHIRE REGIMENT.

(6)

WO 95/2463

34 Division

102 Infantry Brigade

53 Battalion Bedfordshire Regiment

April – July 1919

53 BEDFORDSHIRE REGT

1919 APL — 1919 JLY

Army Form C. 2118.

WAR DIARY
or
INTELLIGENCE SUMMARY. 53rd Battn.

(Erase heading not required.)

Instructions regarding War Diaries and Intelligence Summaries are contained in F.S. Regs., Part II. and the Staff Manual respectively. Title pages will be prepared in manuscript.

Place	Date	Hour	Summary of Events and Information	Remarks and references to Appendices
SIEGBURG	1/4/19		Officer O/Rs Animals	
			Strength 38 1124 (not Batt)	
			Ration do 36 1124 55	
			Detached E. & H.Q. 21 1023	
			Leave 1	
			Hospital 2 39	
			Work begun on "400" range at road	
			2 kilometres N of SIEGBURG. Daily fatigue parties to be detailed by the unit.	
			Capt F L Williams 7/k H.Q. Batting	
			Capt A W Powell	
			L/cpl F Allery of SIEGBURG to HAMAR	
			Cleaning E of SIEGBURG-LOHMAR	
SIEGBURG	2/4/19		Strength on 2/4/19. Scott {Three O.Rs admitted to Hospital	
			Two men departed M.V.S. "sick"	
			2/Lt J.H. Thorley permitted to relinquish commission on account of ill health contained in letter Senne (W.O. letter P.16/22 (M.S.4.k) dated 3.19	

WAR DIARY
or
INTELLIGENCE SUMMARY.
(Erase heading not required.)

Army Form C. 2118.

Instructions regarding War Diaries and Intelligence Summaries are contained in F. S. Regs., Part II. and the Staff Manual respectively. Title pages will be prepared in manuscript.

Place	Date	Hour	Summary of Events and Information	Remarks and references to Appendices
SIEGBURG	3/4/19		Strength Officers O.R Animals 37 1123 55 Incl. M.O and C.F Ration do 34 1015 53 Detached 2 Leave Nil Hospital 2 39 2 Notification received of circulation of Counterfeit notes. Warning issued	
do.	4/4/19		2nd Lt. H. Knight M.C. reported from 1st Northamptonshire Regt.	
do.	5/4/19		Whole Bn. at work on H.C.S. Cregan. 0930 to 1230.	
do.	6/4/19		Reveille + Retreat in future at 0630 and 1930 hrs Notification received of threatened strike in unoccupied Germany. Necessary warning issued.	
do.	7/4/19		Effective Strength Officers O.R Animals 38 1117 55 Ration do 36 1020 54 Detached 2 2 Leave Hospital 2 30 1	

WAR DIARY
or
INTELLIGENCE SUMMARY.

(Erase heading not required.)

Army Form C. 2118.

Instructions regarding War Diaries and Intelligence Summaries are contained in F.S. Regs., Part II. and the Staff Manual respectively. Title pages will be prepared in manuscript.

Place	Date	Hour	Summary of Events and Information	Remarks and references to Appendices
SIEGBURG	8/4/19		E. Strength — Officers 38, O.R. 1115 — Arrivals 56	
			R. do — 36, 1016 — 56	
			Detached — 2, 3	
			Hospital — 2, 32	
do	9/4/19		200 all ranks proceeded on steamer trip BONN – COBLENZ. (PBoats Lyon) reported to HQ 2nd Army, COLOGNE for duty. Major H.A. Hon.	
do	10/4/19		Lecture in SIEGBURGER HOF THEATRE at 10.30 by Lt. Col. L.G. FAWKES R.A on "Royal Army Temperance Association".	
do	11/4/19		Capt L.T.H. LELAND, Worc. R. assumed duties of Brigade Transport Officer. Lieut E.J. DILNUTT BEDFORD R. assumed Command "A" Coy vice Capt L.T.H. LELAND)	
			Lieut ~~L HUMPHREYS~~ ~~MC~~ ~~BEDFORD R~~	
			Lieut L HUMPHREYS. MC BEDFORD R } reported for duty from 11th Bn. SUFFOLK REGT	
			Lieut H.S. SMITH do	
do	12/4/19		E.ff. Strength — Officers 38, O.R. 1110 — Arrivals 55	Brigade Inspected by
			R. do — 37, 1014 — 55	Divisional Commander
			Detached — 4	
			Hospital — 2, 27	

WAR DIARY
or
INTELLIGENCE SUMMARY.

(Erase heading not required.)

Army Form C. 2118.

Place	Date	Hour	Summary of Events and Information	Remarks and references to Appendices
	13/4/19		Capt a/Lt. Col. C.E.G. SHEARMAN DSO. MC. Bedfordshire R. assumed duties of 2nd in Command. Lt. a/Capt. E H GUDGEON) BEDFORDSHIRES reported for duty from 4th Bn BEDFORDSHIRE REGT. AT BLACKETT) REGT.	
	14/4/19		Lieut. J M NAIRN M.C. R.A.S.C.) reported from 4th Bn BEDFORDSHIRE REGT. 2/Lieut. a/Capt. J E VAUGHAN -) BEDFORD REG. 2/Lieut. L G GEARY reported from 1st Bn NORTHAMPTONSHIRE REGT.	
	15/4/19		Having received of proposal to kill all French and British Officers in Occupied GERMANY, and instructions M1 carrying of arms. Orders issued for officers at all times when on duty to carry revolvers whether with or without troops and for O R at all times to wear side arms and when on duty to carry rifles.	
	16/4/19		Col. R D OLDMAN CMG. DSO. assumed command of the Battalion.	
	17/4/19		Eff. Strength Officers OR Animals 47 1106 56 R. do. 42 1002 56 Detached 3 1 Hospital 2 26	

… Army Form C. 2118.

WAR DIARY
or
INTELLIGENCE SUMMARY.
(Erase heading not required.)

Instructions regarding War Diaries and Intelligence Summaries are contained in F. S. Regs., Part II. and the Staff Manual respectively. Title pages will be prepared in manuscript.

Place	Date	Hour	Summary of Events and Information	Remarks and references to Appendices
	18/4/19		Capt J M RYAN R.A.M.C. Evacuated to 103rd Field Ambulance	
	19/4/19		Notification received that Lieut/Capt A N W POWELL transferred to ENGLAND "Sick". Off strength accordingly.	
	20/4/19		Nil	
	21/4/19		Orders received for action to be taken by troops in SIEGBURG in event of civil DISTURBANCE	
	22/4/19		Bn. orders issued re action to be taken in event of civil disturbance	
	23/4/19		Eff. Strength Officers O.R. Animals 46 1105 59 R. do 41 993 59 Detached 3 22 Hospital 2	
	24/4/19		Orders issued re rôle of this unit as reserve batt. (action to be taken / offensive and defensive) in event of resumption of hostilities	
	25/4/19		Warning received re attempts on lives of officers. Guards doubled	
	26/4/19		Guards pltt drilled at night. Lieut A T BLACKETT reported to Brigade H.Q. as Intelligence Officer	

53rd Batt. Bedfordshire Regt.

WAR DIARY
or
INTELLIGENCE SUMMARY.
(Erase heading not required.)

Army Form C. 2118.

Instructions regarding War Diaries and Intelligence Summaries are contained in F.S. Regs., Part II. and the Staff Manual respectively. Title pages will be prepared in manuscript.

Place	Date	Hour	Summary of Events and Information	Remarks and references to Appendices
SIEGBURG	27/4/19		NIL	
do	28/4/19		Intimation received of inspection of this unit by G.O.C. Rhine Army 29/4/19. Warning re. attempt on lives of British & French officers repeated. Orders issued for officers always to carry revolvers when away from their billets	
do	29/4/19		Battalion inspected by General Sir William R. Robertson G.C.B. K.C.V.O. D.S.O. A.D.C. G.O.C in C. British Army of the Rhine. Defence Scheme of 51st & 52nd Bns Bedfordshire Regt. received	
do	30/4/19		Bn. under orders to be ready to move at one hour's notice after 1800 hours -	
do	1/5/19		Bn Tactical exercise. Animals Effective Strength Officers 46 Other Ranks 1106 68 Ration do. 36 979 60 Detached 5 Leave 2 Hospital 18 Bn engaged in Brigade Tactical Exercise. Orders "March Past Posten" issued 0853. Orders to Mass at 1010 hrs. Bn relieved 1600 hours.	
do	1/5/19		Lieut R.C. Morris admitted 57O V.A.H. Bright and sunny	Nil

Army Form C. 2118.

WAR DIARY
or
INTELLIGENCE SUMMARY.
(Erase heading not required.)

Instructions regarding War Diaries and Intelligence Summaries are contained in F. S. Regs., Part II. and the Staff Manual respectively. Title pages will be prepared in manuscript.

Place	Date	Hour	Summary of Events and Information	Remarks and references to Appendices
SIEGBURG	3/4/19		Strength Officers O.R. Animals	
			37 1123 55 Incl. M.O. and C.F.	
			Ration do 34 1015 53	
			Detached 2	
			Leave Nil	
			Hospital 2 39 2	
			Notification received of cancellation of contemplated rail. Warning received	
do	4/4/19		2/Lt. M. Knight M.C. reported from 1st Northamptonshire Regt.	
do	5/4/19		Whole Bn. at work on "dens" aerodrome. 0930 to 1230.	
do	6/4/19		Revielle - Church - Juttes at 0830 and 1930 by Notification received of Armistice Strike in occupied Germany. Necessary warning issued	
do	7/4/19		Officers O.R. Animals	
			Whole Strength 38 1117 55	
			Ration do 36 1020 52	
			Detached 2 2	
			Leave	
			Hospital 2 30 1	

Army Form C. 2118.

WAR DIARY
or
INTELLIGENCE SUMMARY.
(Erase heading not required.)

Instructions regarding War Diaries and Intelligence Summaries are contained in F.S. Regs., Part II. and the Staff Manual respectively. Title pages will be prepared in manuscript.

Place	Date	Hour	Summary of Events and Information	Remarks and references to Appendices
SIEGBURG	8/4/19		Officers O R Animals E. Strength 38 1115 56 R do 36 1016 56 Detached 2 3 Hospital 2 32	
do.	9/4/19		200 all ranks proceeded on steamer trip BONN – COBLENZ Major H.W. P Bowes Lofson reported to HQ 2 Army, COLOGNE for duty.	
do.	10/4/19		Lecture in SIEG-BURGER HOF THEATRE at 10.30 by Lt. Ed. L G FEWKES R.A. on "Royal Army Temperance Association"	
do	11/4/19		Capt. L.T.H. LELAND WORK. R. assumed duties of Brigade Transport Officer Lieut. E.J. DILNUTT BEDFORD R. assumed command "A" Coy v/c Capt L.T.H. LELAND Lieut L HUMPHREYS. M.C. BEDFORD R.} reported for duty from 11th Bn. SUFFOLK REGT Lieut H.S. SMITH do	
do	12/4/19		Officers OR Animals Eff Strength 38 1110 55 R do 37 1014 55 Detached 4 Hospital 2 27	Brigade Inspection by Divisional Commander.

Army Form C. 2118.

WAR DIARY
or
INTELLIGENCE SUMMARY.
(Erase heading not required.)

Instructions regarding War Diaries and Intelligence Summaries are contained in F.S. Regs., Part II. and the Staff Manual respectively. Title pages will be prepared in manuscript.

Place	Date	Hour	Summary of Events and Information	Remarks and references to Appendices
	13/4/19		Capt a/Lt. Col. C.E.G. SHEARMAN DSO MC Bedfordshire R. resumed duties of 2nd in Command. Lt. %Capt. E.H. GUDGEON Bedfordshires reported from duty from 4th Bn. BEDFORDSHIRE REGT. AT BLACKETT	
	14/4/19		Lieut. J.M. NAIRN M.C. } reported from 4th Bn. BEDFORDSHIRE REGT. 2Lieut. a/Capt. J.E. VAUGHAN Bedford R. 2Lieut. L.G. GERRY reported from 1st Bn. NORTHAMPTONSHIRE REGT.	
	15/4/19		Warning received of proposal to kill all French and British Officers in Occupied GERMANY, and construction M carrying of arms. Orders issued for officers at all times when on duty, to carry revolver with or without troops and for O.R. at all times to wear side arms and when on duty to carry rifles.	
	16/4/19		Col. R.D. OLDMAN CMG DSO. assumed command of the Battalion.	
	17/4/19			
			Officers O.R. Animals	
			Eff. Strength 47 1106 57	
			R. do. 42 1002 57	
			Detached 3 1	
			Hospital 2 26	

Army Form C. 2118.

WAR DIARY
or
INTELLIGENCE SUMMARY.
(Erase heading not required.)

Instructions regarding War Diaries and Intelligence Summaries are contained in F. S. Regs., Part II. and the Staff Manual respectively. Title pages will be prepared in manuscript.

Place	Date	Hour	Summary of Events and Information	Remarks and references to Appendices
	18/4/19		Capt J M RYAN R.A.M.C. Medical Off. 6/103rd Field Ambulance	
	19/4/19		Notification received that Lieut /Capt A M W POWELL transferred to ENGLAND Sick. Off strength accordingly.	
	20/4/19		NIL	
	21/4/19		Orders received for action to be taken by troops in SIEGBURG in event of Civil Disturbance	
	22/4/19		Bn. orders issued re action to be taken in event of such disturbance	
	23/4/19		Strength: Officers O.R. Animals HQ 46 1105 59 R do 41 943 59 Detached 3 Hospital 2 22	
	24/4/19		Orders issued re rôle of the unit as percent shelter. Action to be taken (offensive and defensive) in event of disruption of hostilities	
	25/4/19		Warning received re attempts on lives of officers - Guards doubled.	
	26/4/19		Guards platoon doubled at night. Lieut AT BLACKETT reported to Brigade HQ as Intelligence Officer	

Army Form C. 2118.

WAR DIARY
or
INTELLIGENCE SUMMARY.
(Erase heading not required.)

Instructions regarding War Diaries and Intelligence Summaries are contained in F. S. Regs., Part II. and the Staff Manual respectively. Title pages will be prepared in manuscript.

Place	Date	Hour	Summary of Events and Information	Remarks and references to Appendices
SIEGBURG	2/5/19		2/Lieut G.H.D Adams admitted 67th F.A.	
	3/5/19		Bright. Sunny. - NIL -	
do.	4/5/19		- NIL -	
do.	5/5/19		- NIL -	
do.	6/5/19		- NIL -	
do.	7/5/19		London Gazette Supplement 2/Lieut G.H.D Adams to be Lieut. (Dec 27th 1918)	
	8/5/19		Bn. on Tactical Scheme - SEULGENTHAL	
	9/5/19			
	10/5/19			
	11/5/19		Reveille in future at 0630. Reveal 2030 hrs. 2/Lieut E.J. Smith reported to ADRT Cslo a.a.	
	12/5/19			
	13/5/19		Capt E.M. Cugell proceed B.U.K. Struck off streng ? according (Cmtry:-) G.H.Q AG 8638(a) d. 30.3.19. Lieut Adams discharged from hospital	
	14/5/19		Bn. School opened. Farriers M'Gair NCi.o. van kleg, Levan NCi. Commandant Lieut H.S Gray.	(1)

Army Form C. 2118.

WAR DIARY
or
INTELLIGENCE SUMMARY.
(Erase heading not required.)

Place	Date	Hour	Summary of Events and Information	Remarks and references to Appendices
SIEGBURG	15/5/19		Bright and Sunny	
do	16/5/19		Hours of Training altered to avoid heat of day:— Reveille 0600. Breakfast 0630. Training 0730-1200. Dinner 1215. Voluntary Education 1400-1600. Tea 1600. Games 1600-2000. Grand Rounds 1930. Lights out 2200. Bright and Sunny	
do	17/5/19		Major Hon. P. Bowes Lyon struck off strength on appointment as Secretary, Officers Sports Club. (G.H.Q. No. G.E. 22/11 Inf. Bde. A20/62d. 16/5/19.) Warning order received of anticipated relief & move to WAHN 31/5/19 Very hot	
do	18/5/19		Lieut. H. Tolhurst admitted to 104" F.A. Very fine.	
do	19/5/19		Very fine. Notification received that Relief / Brigade would not take place until 14/6/19 (Civie)	
	20/5/19		Very fine..	
	21/5/19		Very fine. Rear guard issued naval movements whether Germans would accept peace terms	
	22/5/19		Orders issued Entg (Preparations) advance. Lieut. Humphrey. M.C. reported to 2Bn L.T.M.B. for duty. A Coy out on "Stunts" owing to outbreak of mumps. Very fine.	

Army Form C. 2118.

WAR DIARY
or
INTELLIGENCE SUMMARY.
(Erase heading not required.)

Instructions regarding War Diaries and Intelligence Summaries are contained in F. S. Regs., Part II. and the Staff Manual respectively. Title pages will be prepared in manuscript.

Place	Date	Hour	Summary of Events and Information	Remarks and references to Appendices
SIEGBURG	23/5/19		Very fine. Orders received from Bde No action to be taken in event of Peace Terms not being signed.	
do.	24/5/19		Weather unchanged. Battalion Stores Relief.	
do.	25/5/19		Weather unchanged.	
do.	26/5/19		Further orders received reg action to be taken in event of Peace Terms not being signed. A.B. Coys begin firing G.M.C. Some artillery fire thro'out SIEGBURG to outpost line. Weather unchanged until 1900 hrs. Some rain then.	
do.	27/5/19		NIL Very few	
do.	28/5/19		Lieut L. L. Humphreys M.C. taken on strength of 2nd L.T.M.B. Off Strength of this unit accordingly. (Auth. - 2nd Bde No Q 1795 - d 27.5.19. Weather unchanged.	
do.	29/5/19		Weather unchanged. Notification received (2nd Bde A/1/1 d 28/5/19) that Lieut A.T. BLACKETT on strength of 2nd Bde H.Q. Coy from 4/5/19. Off Strength accordingly. Lieut F. ALLEN and 2nd Lieut E.J. SMYTH transferred to 4th Bn SUFFOLK REGT. (Authy Eastern Divisn No. A 4069 d 25/5/19 Lieut H.J. LORD to assume Command of C Coy during absence on leave of Lieut E. KINNEAD M.C. 31/5/19 to 14/6/19	

Army Form C. 2118.

WAR DIARY
or
INTELLIGENCE SUMMARY.
(Erase heading not required.)

Place	Date	Hour	Summary of Events and Information	Remarks and references to Appendices
SIEGBURG	30/4/19		Weather unchanged.	
	3/5/19		Weather unchanged. Further Particulars received re billets & water supplies in country through which actual advance will take place, if troops home are not required. Lieut. H. KNIGHT M.C. Bedfordshire Regt. (Proceeded to U K for demobilisation Authy: – Rhine Army No A93/17(61) d 26.5.19)	

WAR DIARY or INTELLIGENCE SUMMARY

5BD BN BEDFORDSHIRE REGT

Army Form C. 2118.

Place	Date	Hour	Summary of Events and Information	Remarks and references to Appendices
SIEGBURG	1/6/19		Weather unchanged.	
			Strength	
			Offs. Other Ranks Animals	
			Effective Strength 39 1107 55	
			Ration do 37* 983 55 *Inclusive 3 R.E. Officers att.	
			Departed 2 for action.	
			Leave 1 7	
			Hospital 4 43	
do.	2/6/19		Notification received that Col. R.J. Barker C.M.G. D.S.O. ceased to struck off strength as from 6/3/19 on assuming Command 53rd Bn. R. Sussex Regt. (Please Army No. AA6/64 of 4/3/19)	
do.	3/6/19		King's Birthday. Ceremonial Parade at 0930 hrs. Holiday. Weather changed - rain during day.	
do.	4/6/19.		Col. R.D.F. OLDMAN C.M.G. D.S.O. proceed E.U.K on leave. Major C.E.G. SHEPHERD D.S.O. M.C. assumes command of Bn. Major D.N. ROWE 2nd in Command.	

Army Form C. 2118.

WAR DIARY
or
INTELLIGENCE SUMMARY.
(Erase heading not required.)

Instructions regarding War Diaries and Intelligence Summaries are contained in F. S. Regs., Part II. and the Staff Manual respectively. Title pages will be prepared in manuscript.

Place	Date	Hour	Summary of Events and Information	Remarks and references to Appendices
SIEGBURG	4/6/19		Bn Orders issued 12 noon on 3rd day	
do	5/6/19		Rain throughout day.	
do	6/6/19		Lieut R.C. Morris discharged from 29th C.C.S.	
do	7/6/19		Nil	
do	8/6/19		Instructions re Discipline on Calais Leave Service. Brigadier's Horse Show	
do	9/6/19		Brigade's Horse Show - Sof th Sieg opposite Weingartgasse 1400 hrs. Office of Divis Cashier closes on Saturdays 12.30 pm re-opens Mondays 09.30 hrs. Good lending library & Book Shop under auspices of Y.M.C.A. located over A.P.O. Munster Platz, Bonn. Can be used by both Officers & men.	
do	10/6/19		Branch of War Savings Association formed in Battn.	
do	11/6/19		Vacancies allotted for S/Seamen trip Bonn - Coblenz & Coy 20 B Coy 70 & C Coy 30. Transport 12. First & Second Prize for Best Essay & Best Photograph. Lieut Dilnutt CSM Coulson & Sgt Ingrey watched Artillery practice at WAHN. Lecture given by Rev. C.A. Heacott. B.A. on Browning Diocese Cinema Hall Siegburg. G.H.Q. F.S.O. opens for General Business Week-days 0800 to 1300 & 1400 to 1930. Sundays 0800 to 1300.	

A6945. Wt. W14422/M1160 350,000 12/16 D. D. & L. Forms/C.2118/14.

WAR DIARY or INTELLIGENCE SUMMARY.

Army Form C. 2118.

Place	Date	Hour	Summary of Events and Information	Remarks and references to Appendices
Siegburg	12/6/19		Lieut W. Tolhurst evacuated to O.K. 6.6.19. Sick. Baggage allowance increased from 1½ cwt to 3 cwt in case of British Officers of all Arms proceeding to or forming part of Army of Occupation.	
do	13/6/19		O.C. C Coy. detailed 1 Officer 3 Sgt. to watch Artillery Practice Wahn.	
do	13/6/19		Rev. R. Mowray reported to Battalion 13/3/19 for duty as Roman Catholic Chaplain.	
do	14/6/19		Nil	
do	15/6/19		Nil	
do	16/6/19		Entries for 51st Bedfords Rifle Sports closed 12.00 hrs. Altenrath Rifle Range – Winners in Class "A" Buid Competitions week ending 14/6/19	
			1st Competition	
			1st 26025 Sgt. J. Ingrey A Coy	A Coy
			2nd 66760 Sgt. a. J. Wingfield D.C.M. M.M. A Coy	A Coy
			2nd Competition	
			1st (tiers between) {23124 O.R.S. P.K. Munn 26025 Sgt. J. Ingrey.	A Coy A Coy
			2nd. 66760 Sgt. J. Wingfield. D.C.M. M.M.	A Coy

Army Form C. 2118.

WAR DIARY
or
INTELLIGENCE SUMMARY.
(Erase heading not required.)

Instructions regarding War Diaries and Intelligence Summaries are contained in F. S. Regs., Part II. and the Staff Manual respectively. Title pages will be prepared in manuscript.

Place	Date	Hour	Summary of Events and Information	Remarks and references to Appendices
Siegburg	17/6/19		Received information that 3rd day would be Friday 20th June 1919.	
do	18/6/19		Rhine trips. No objection to Officers & other Ranks taking pleasure trips on Steamers for civilians. They will pay the normal fares charged to civilians. Major S. White Northumberland Regt reports for duty. Posted to 'C' Coy. Sgt Bosford Regt Spots Paymaster Cologne in Cheques Healey Siegburg at 1800 hrs for the new system of Pay Week Books. All Coy Commanders – Cam's attached. Cancelled.	postpone will posn later. I say
do	19/6/19		Officers proceeding on leave to London should obtain Hotel Cards before leaving Boulogne - owing to difficulty of obtaining accommodation. Lt. S. Sydlin-Union reports for duty at Army Technical College Siegburg + Commas attack accordingly. Col. R. M. F. Oldman C.M.G., D.S.O. returns from leave to U.K.	
do	20/6/19		Major C.E.G. Shearman D.S.O. M.C. reports to Eastern Division for duty to cease attachment accordingly. All Ranks warned re Cannock Training Range Spirits.	
do	21/6/19		Tactical Demonstration by N.C.O's School under the Commanding Officer all officers attended.	

Army Form C. 2118.

WAR DIARY
or
INTELLIGENCE SUMMARY.
(Erase heading not required.)

Instructions regarding War Diaries and Intelligence Summaries are contained in F. S. Regs., Part II. and the Staff Manual respectively. Title pages will be prepared in manuscript.

Place	Date	Hour	Summary of Events and Information	Remarks and references to Appendices
Siegburg	21/6/19		Lieut. C.J. Grant reports to No 16 R.S.D. for duty with A.S.S. recom attachment accordingly.	
			All personnel returning from leave will pass through Divisional Reception Camp.	
			Captain Gibbs, Lieut Hunter & 2/Lieut Irish R.E. cease attachment to this Unit for Rations 20.6.1919 inclusive.	
			Payment to troops will continue on A.B.64 acquittance rolls until further orders.	
do	22/6/19		Nil.	
do	23/6/19		Inter Inter-Platoon Cross-Country Run. 1st. No 16 Platoon B Coy. 2nd No. 6 Platoon B Coy.	
do	24/6/19		No 16 Platoon to represent Battalion in 2nd Platoon Cross Country Run.	
do	25/6/19		Orders re move to Wahn received. Advance baggage loaded.	
do	26/6/19		Advance Party 3 officers & 60 O.R. proceeded to HAHN O'Clock. Leave Service timings received. Rates of Exchange from 10.30 h. 23. 6. 1919 10 marks = 7/9 5 francs (French) 3/5 5 francs " 2/4. (X Corps R.O. 3957 dated 25. 6. 1919.	

WAR DIARY
or
INTELLIGENCE SUMMARY.
(Erase heading not required.)

Army Form C. 2118.

Place	Date	Hour	Summary of Events and Information	Remarks and references to Appendices
Siegburg	26/6/19		Instructions re damage to Railways received.	
—	27/6/19		Col. R.A.J. Oldman, C.M.G. D.S.O. granted leave to U.K. from 27.6.19 - 14.7.19. Major D.N. Rowe assumed command of the Battalion during absence of Lt. Col. Oldman C.M.G. D.S.O.	
	28/6/19		Peace signed with Germany at Versailles.	
—	29/6/19		Buses arrived for Wahn. Received Major Skeavan D.S.O. M.C. reports from arrival drug refresher command of the Battalion vice Major D.N. Rowe.	
—	30/6/19		Battalion moved to Wahn - left Siegburg 14.10 hrs arrived Wahn 17.00 hrs	

Army Form C. 2118.

of 53rd Battn. Bedfordshire Regt.

WAR DIARY
or
INTELLIGENCE SUMMARY.
(Erase heading not required.)

Instructions regarding War Diaries and Intelligence Summaries are contained in F. S. Regs., Part II. and the Staff Manual respectively. Title pages will be prepared in manuscript.

Place	Date	Hour	Summary of Events and Information	Remarks and references to Appendices
WAHN	1/7/19		Capt. Mann, R.A.M.C. reported for duty as M.O. Lieut. R.C. Morris proceeded to No1 Rect Camp Cologne for Demobilisation 29/6/19. Leave of office of the unit stopped owing to demand line Command SIEGBURG. 29/6/19.	
—	2/7/19		Attention drawn to Forgis Passes. (IX Corps. R.O. No: 3982 dated 30th June 1919.)	
—	3/7/19		General Holiday for all the troops of Rhine Army to Commemorate the signing of the Peace Treaty.	
—	4/7/19		2nd Class Army Certificate Examinations	
—	5/7/19		3rd Class Army Certificate Examinations	
—	6/7/19		Special Units Thanksgiving Service to celebrate signing of the Peace Treaty.	
—	7/7/19		NIL	
	8/7/19		NIL	
	9/7/19		NIL	
	10/7/19		NIL	
	11/7/19		NIL	
	12/7/19		NIL	
	13/7/19		Owing to outbreak of Typhoid Fever ALTENAHR placed on R.A.H.R. E. out to REMAGEN out of bounds.	
	14/7/19		Notification received of two/three arrivals of British troops against German civilians are to be punished. Orders received to	

WAR DIARY
or
INTELLIGENCE SUMMARY.
(Erase heading not required.)

Army Form C. 2118.

Instructions regarding War Diaries and Intelligence Summaries are contained in F. S. Regs., Part II. and the Staff Manual respectively. Title pages will be prepared in manuscript.

Place	Date	Hour	Summary of Events and Information	Remarks and references to Appendices
	15.7.19		Cadre Staffs to present Same.	
	16.7.19		Col. R.D.F. OLDMAN CMG. D.S.O. returned from leave and resumed command. Rhine Trip to COBLENZ. 190 vacancies allotted this unit.	
	17.7.19		Battn. Sports held.	
	18.7.19		Battalion participate in Brigade Tactical Exercise	
	19.7.19		General holiday owing to Celebration of Peace.	
	20.7.19		NIL	
	21.7.19		Battalion NIL.	
	22.7.19		Battalion participate in Brigade Tactical Exercise	
	23.7.19		First Class Army Certificate Examination held	
			First Class Army Certificate Examination	
	24.7.19		do.	
	25.7.19		Brigade Sports held	
			NIL -	
	26.7.19		Major C.E.G. SHEARMAN D.S.O. M.C. reported to H.Q. Eastern Division for duty.	
	27.7.19		NIL -	

WAR DIARY
or
INTELLIGENCE SUMMARY.
(Erase heading not required.)

Army Form C. 2118.

Place	Date	Hour	Summary of Events and Information	Remarks and references to Appendices
	28.7.19	1000	Bn inspected by Brig.- Genl. H.C. JACKSON C.B. D.S.O	
		1400	Memorial Service for Officers W.O's N.C.O's & men of the BEDFORDSHIRE REGT. who fell in action in the War held in Camp Church WAHN – simultaneously with similar service held in ST. PAUL'S CHURCH BEDFORD. 220 from each Battalion of the Brigade attended.	
	29.7.19		Battalion on Brigade Tactical Exercise.	
	30.7.19		Battalion on Battalion Tactical Exercise.	
	31.7.19		Holiday owing to Divisional Horse Show held at SIEGBURG. Notification received that all leave for Eastern Division was stopped. All General Officers Commanding Officers & Staff Officers to be recalled from leave. Authority received for striking Capt. J.M. RYAN R.A.M.C. off strength of this unit (2nd Ech. A24/30 d. 3/7/19)	

Army Form C. 2118.

WAR DIARY
or
INTELLIGENCE SUMMARY.
(Erase heading not required.)

Instructions regarding War Diaries and Intelligence Summaries are contained in F. S. Regs., Part II. and the Staff Manual respectively. Title pages will be prepared in manuscript.

Place	Date	Hour	Summary of Events and Information	Remarks and references to Appendices
WAHN	1/7/19		Capt. Kearns reports for duty as M.O. Lieut. R.C. Morrow proceeded to No.1 Receipt Camp Cologne for Demobilization (ref 2018/19 - Ind office letter (19a) misc. G.120/20 dtd 29/6/19	
—	2/7/19		Attention drawn to Army Routine (K. Corps R.O. no 3982 dated 24 June 1919.)	
—	3/7/19		General Holiday for all the troops of Rhine Army to commemorate the signing of the Peace Treaty	
—	4/7/19		2nd Class Army Certificate Examinations	
—	5/7/19		3rd Class Army Certificate Examinations	
—	6/7/19		Special Allied Thanksgiving Service to celebrate signing of the Peace Treaty	
—	7/7/19		Nil	
—	8/7/19		Nil	
—	9/7/19		Nil	
—	10/7/19		Nil	
—	11/7/19		Nil	
	12/7/19		Coy 1 entrained for Tilburg midnight hence 12.R. & Lt REMAGEN of which	
	13/7/19		Nil. also received of Montreal of march by Bicklof of Capt. exchange	
	14/7/19		Lt. Friendel Eleven gilt of Crossing into Capt. Butler account to	

A6945 Wt. W14142/M1160 350,000 12/16 D. D. & L. Forms/C./2118/14.

WAR DIARY
or
INTELLIGENCE SUMMARY.
(Erase heading not required.)

Army Form C. 2118.

Instructions regarding War Diaries and Intelligence Summaries are contained in F. S. Regs., Part II. and the Staff Manual respectively. Title pages will be prepared in manuscript.

Place	Date	Hour	Summary of Events and Information	Remarks and references to Appendices
	15/7/19		Lake Steps Expenent Scene.	
	16/7/19		Col. RDF OLDMAN CMG DSO returned from leave and resumed command	
	17/7/19		RHQ T.4 to COBLENZ. 90 horses are allotted this unit.	
	18/7/19		Batt. Sports held	
	19/7/19		Battalion participate in Brigade Tactical Exercise	
	20/7/19		Funeral Infantry Corp of Catholics of Personnel	
	21/7/19		NIL	
	22/7/19		Attention NIL	
	23/7/19		Battalion participated in Brigade Tactical Exercise	
	23/7/19		First Class Army Certificates Examination held	
	24/7/19		First Class Army Cert of Education held	
	25/7/19		do	
	26/7/19		Brigade Sports held	
	27/7/19		NIL	
	28/7/19		Major C.E.G. SHEARMAN DSO MC attached to H.Q. Eastern Division for duty	
	29/7/19		NIL	

Army Form C. 2118.

WAR DIARY
or
INTELLIGENCE SUMMARY.
(Erase heading not required.)

Instructions regarding War Diaries and Intelligence Summaries are contained in F. S. Regs., Part II. and the Staff Manual respectively. Title pages will be prepared in manuscript.

Place	Date	Hour	Summary of Events and Information	Remarks and references to Appendices
	28.7.19	1000	Presented by Brig. Genl H.C. JACKSON C.B. D.S.O.	
		1100	Memorial Service for Officers NCOs & men of the BEDFORDSHIRE Regt. who fell in action in the War held in Gt Chart WARR — previous service held in ST PAULS CHURCH BEDFORD. 220 Officers and men of 1st Battalion of 15th Brigade attended.	
	29.7.19		Battalion on Brigade Tactical Exercise	
	30.7.19		Battalion on Battalion Tactical Exercise	
	31.7.19		Holiday owing to Dominion Horse Show held at SIEGBURG. Notification received that all leave for Eastern Division was stopped. All General Officers Commanding Officers & Staff Officers to be recalled from leave. Authority received for striking Capt J M RYAN name off strength of the unit. (2nd Bn A2W/30 dt 29/7/19)